D0745453

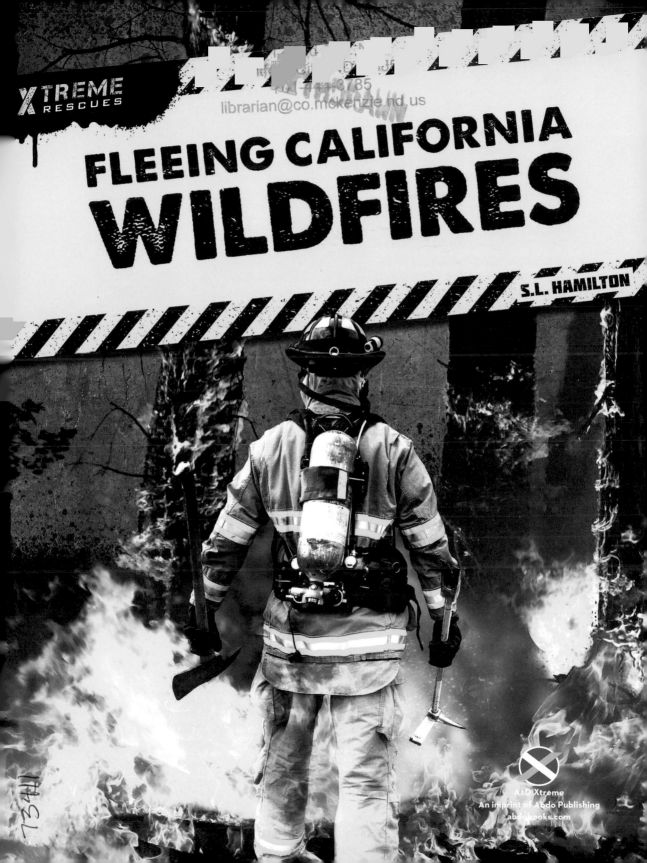

XTREME RESCUES

FLEEING CALIFORNIA
WILDFIRES

S.L. HAMILTON

A&D Xtreme
An imprint of Abdo Publishing
abdobooks.com

abdobooks.com

Published by Abdo Publishing, a division of ABDO,
PO Box 398166, Minneapolis, Minnesota 55439.

Printed in the United States of America, North Mankato, MN.
092019
012020

THIS BOOK CONTAINS
RECYCLED MATERIALS

Editor: John Hamilton
Copy Editor: Bridget O'Brien
Graphic Design: Sue Hamilton & Dorothy Toth
Cover Design: Victoria Bates
Cover Photo: Alamy
Interior Photos & Illustrations: Alamy-pg 1; AP-pgs 4-5, 12-13, 14-15, 18-19, 22-23 & 24-25; Bureau of Land
Management California-pgs 6-7, 28-29 & 30-31; Getty Images-pgs 10-11, 16-17 & 20-21; Los Angeles Fire
Department/David Nordquist-pgs 26-27; Shutterstock-pg 32; US Forest Service-pgs 2-3 & 8-9.

Library of Congress Control Number: 2019941934
Publisher's Cataloging-in-Publication Data

Names: Hamilton, S.L., author.
Title: Fleeing California wildfires / by S.L. Hamilton
Description: Minneapolis, Minnesota : Abdo Publishing, 2020 | Series: Xtreme rescues | Includes online
    resources and index.
Identifiers: ISBN 9781532190025 (lib. bdg.) | ISBN 9781644943502 (pbk.) | ISBN 9781532175879 (ebook)
Subjects: LCSH: Wildfires--California--Juvenile literature. | Natural disasters--Juvenile literature. | Disaster
    relief--California--Juvenile literature. | Migration--Climatic factors--Juvenile literature. | Migration,
    Internal--United States--Juvenile literature.
Classification: DDC 363.34--dc23

CONTENTS

WILDFIRES

In 2018, California had little rain, strong winds, dead trees, and dry bushes. These conditions resulted in the worst wildfire season of all time. That year's wildfires caused the greatest number of acres burned, the most deaths, and the largest number of buildings destroyed. Firefighters and police, as well as members of the US Forest Service and National Guard, search and rescue personnel, and brave citizens worked together to help rescue people and animals while fighting the raging flames.

XTREME FACT

Before the Fires

By 2018, California had suffered years of drought and a record number of dead trees caused by bark beetles. The state also faced high heat, low humidity, and strong winds. Conditions were right for a deadly fire season.

A firefighter wets down dry brush in areas at risk for wildfires.

XTREME FACT

Humans cause about 90 percent of wildfires. Lightning causes about 10 percent.

THE WORLD FINDS OUT

Public knowledge of California's wildfires spread as fast as the flames. The state has a wildfire season every year from spring to late fall. Early in 2018, the wildfire season became one of the worst ever. Several burned areas of California were already declared national disasters by August 2018.

Smoke from a 2018 California wildfire billows out to the coast.

FIRES SPREAD IN WILDLANDS

Homes were built in wildlands as California's population grew over the years. Wildlands are areas with little development. Many times only a single road leads to the area. Wildlands often have a lot of trees and vegetation that are perfect fuel for fires.

Flames spread across a home and over the road in Paradise, California.

Several of the 2018 fires spread fast in wildland areas. Sometimes, citizens had little warning before the flames were upon them. Everyone tried to escape at the same time. Vehicles clogged the few roads. Many people were trapped in their cars and towns.

Go Now!

As the flames grew, it became clear that firefighters would be unable to stop the fires from reaching some towns. Flames licked at the roads. People were told to "Go now!"

Firefighters try to keep flames from engulfing a road.

ESCAPING IN VEHICLES

Because the fires spread so fast, hundreds of people had to leave their homes at the same time. People got in their vehicles and fled. This caused terrible traffic jams. Suddenly, citizens of burning towns were trapped on roads in the middle of raging flames, thick smoke, and stalled or abandoned vehicles.

XTREME QUOTE

"You could hear the explosions from people's vehicle tires popping from the heat." —California Camp Fire Survivor

ESCAPING ON FOOT

Sometimes the only way to escape the flames was to walk or run away. Roads were often blocked by emergency vehicles, downed power lines, and broken tree branches.

Abandoned, burned-out cars and downed power lines border the main road near Paradise, California.

Some people parked their cars by the side of the road and fled on foot. High winds blew fiery sparks, hot ash, smoke, and flames at those trying to escape. People often had only the clothes on their backs to protect themselves.

GROUND RESCUE TEAMS

People trapped by fast-moving flames needed help to escape. Hundreds of firefighters from California and other states risked their lives to beat back the 2018 wildfires. Many people made it out because firefighters used all their skills to keep the roads open.

ANIMAL RESCUES

California farmers and ranchers faced a difficult situation. With the wildfires upon them, they had to leave or be killed. This left their animals unprotected. People watered the areas around their animals' shelters, and hoped for a miracle. Sometimes animals were let loose so they could try to outrun the flames.

Sometimes calls went out for help. People with trucks and trailers drove into danger to load up and rescue horses, llamas, goats, and other large animals. However, roads needed to stay open for firefighting equipment and personnel to do their jobs. It was a difficult choice to allow animal rescues or to stop the trucks and trailers and know that animals might die.

Sheriff's deputies evacuate horses at risk from a California fire.

Aerial Firefighting and Rescues

California rescues were aided by air attacks. Specially designed helicopters and fixed-wing aircraft carried hundreds of gallons of water or red fire-retardant chemicals. Pilots flew into smoke and dangerous winds to drop these fire-suppressing loads. This slowed the advancing flames and gave people a chance to escape.

Helicopters fitted with tanks or buckets were also used to help stop flames from spreading. The water-carrying helicopters stayed close to the spreading fires by filling up at nearby lakes. If a helicopter delivered firefighters and their equipment to a fire line, it was called a "helitack."

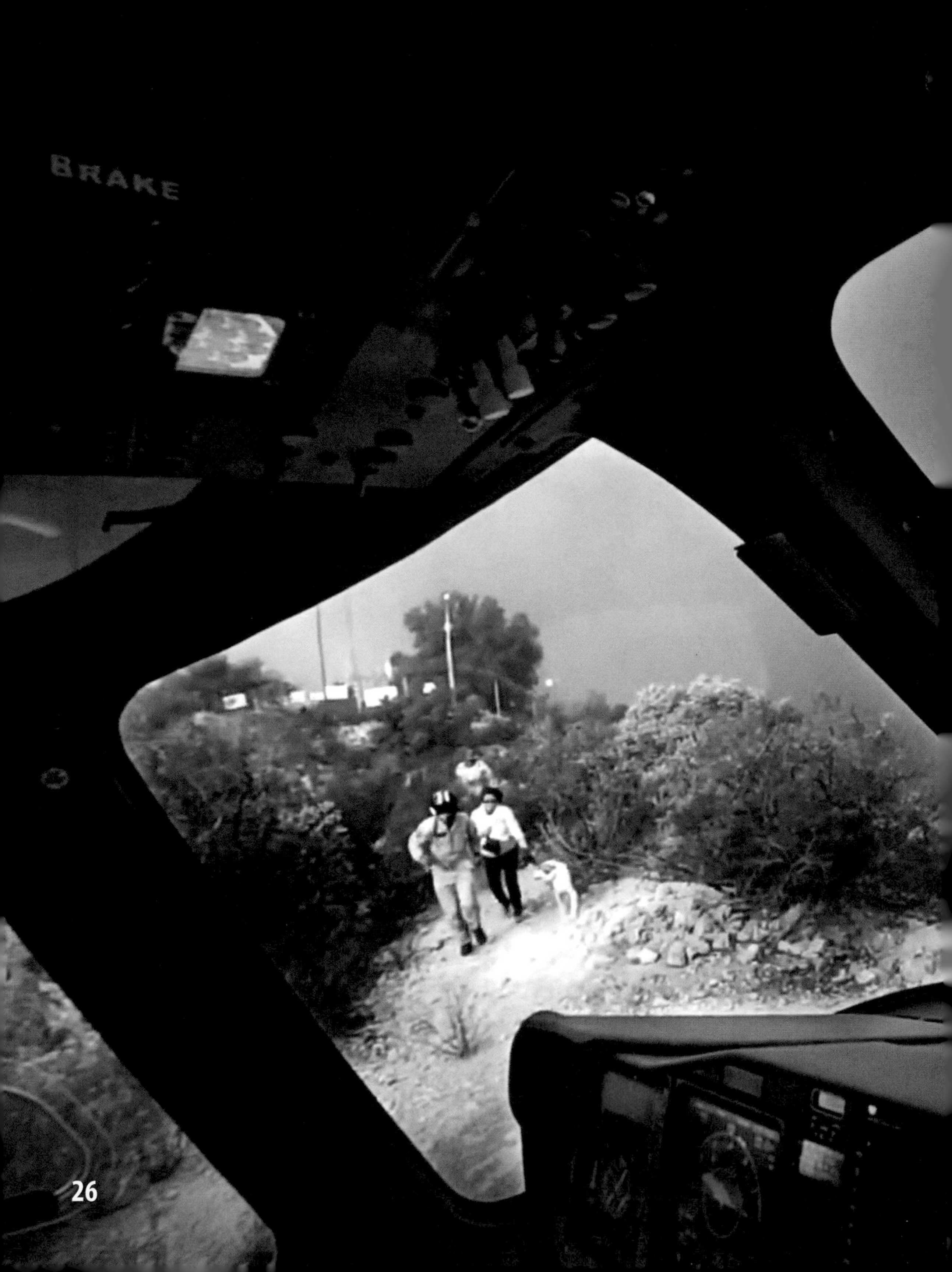
BRAKE

Fire travels quickly uphill. Some Californians were trapped by fire and smoke on steep hills and mountaintops. Helicopter teams were called to rescue these people. Sometimes pilots hovered above, dropped rescue baskets, and hoisted citizens to safety. Other times, helicopter pilots dodged buildings, trees, and power lines to make very dangerous landings to rescue people and pets.

Los Angeles Fire Department Air Operations pilots rescue a trapped family from the Woolsey Fire on November 9, 2018, in Malibu, California.

WHAT IF IT HAPPENS TO YOU?

The most important factor in surviving a wildfire is to stay calm, but get out quickly. If you see fire or smoke, leave the area. Wildfires move fast.

If Trapped In Your Home. . .
• Call 911 and let officials know where you are.
• Stay inside, but away from outside walls and windows.
• Wear cotton or wool clothing. Synthetics can melt on you.
• Close all doors and windows, but keep them unlocked.
• Be ready to leave quickly when rescuers arrive.

If Trapped In A Vehicle. . .
- Call 911 and let officials know where you are.
- Have the driver park far from trees and plants.
- Close all vents, so smoke cannot enter.
- Lie on the floor with a wool coat or blanket over you. Or put a bandanna or other piece of clothing over your nose and mouth to filter out the smoke.

No matter where you are, follow the directions of fire officials. They will give you the best advice for survival. Remember that homes and objects can be replaced, but lives cannot.

The 2018 Carr Fire burned more than 1,000 homes.

GLOSSARY

ABANDONED
Something that has purposely been left behind by its owner.

BANDANNA
A square scarf that is usually folded at an angle and tied around the head, face, or neck for protection.

BARK BEETLES
Insects that eat tree bark. Bark beetles often attack and kill trees that are already stressed, such as during droughts.

DROUGHT
When an area receives much less rain than it normally does for an extended amount of time.

FIRE-RETARDANT CHEMICALS
A combination of water, fertilizer, thickener (such as clay), and iron oxide (which gives it the red color) spread by a firefighting aircraft. It keeps a fire from spreading so firefighters have time to get to the location and people can escape. Although mostly water, the added fertilizer helps plants regrow in burned areas. The thickener keeps the water from quickly evaporating in high heat and wind. The red color shows where it was dropped.

Fixed-Wing Aircraft
Planes with wings fixed in place. Helicopters have rotary wings that move.

National Disaster
When an event, such as a fire, storm, or other force of nature, causes so much damage or loss of life, that money from the US government is used to help the people and businesses affected by the disaster.

National Guard
Citizen soldiers who are trained members of the US Army and Air Force, organized as units by state. They may be called in to serve during local and national emergencies.

Stall
During a fire, when smoke, heat, and ash stop a vehicle's engine from running. The vehicle will not go.

Synthetic Clothing
Clothing made from artificial, chemically-created materials. This is the opposite of clothing made from naturally grown materials (such as wool or cotton).

Vegetation
All plant life, such as trees, plants, and brush.

Online Resources

Booklinks
NONFICTION NETWORK
FREE! ONLINE NONFICTION RESOURCES

To learn more about fleeing California wildfires, visit abdobooklinks.com or scan this QR code. These links are routinely monitored and updated to provide the most current information available.

INDEX